HomeLink
READERS
3

Authors

Mario Herrera and

Theresa Zanatta

Longman

Contents

HomeLink Readers 3 Art Reader 1, Roni Shepherd; Reader 2, Caroline Merola; Reader 3, Chris Demarest; Reader 4, Jenny Vainisi; Reader 5, Rose Mary Berlin; Reader 6, Steven Wolfgang; Reader 7, Marsha Winborn; Reader 8, Hrana Janto; Reader 9, Manuel King.

HomeLink Readers 3

Pearson Education, 10 Bank Street, White Plains, NY 10606

Cover design: Pearson Education Development Group
Cover art: Jenny Vainisi
Text design: Pearson Education Development Group

ISBN: 0-13-028370-3
    4 5 6 7 8 9 10—BAM—05 04 03

The Ant and the Grasshopper

Based on a Fable

Retold by Yoko Mia Hirano

Ant lives next to Grasshopper. Ant says, "I like to work and go to school every day."

Every day Ant gets up at 7:15. She finds food before school. She reads and writes.

After school she plays soccer.

Ant works and works. Grasshopper doesn't like to work.

Grasshopper looks at Ant's food. "Can I eat some of your food?" she asks.

Ant says, "I work every day. You hop and sing and play."

Grasshopper says, "After lunch, I can work." Ant gives Grasshopper some food.

After lunch Grasshopper hops and sings and works!

One day Grasshopper gets up at 10:00. She says, "I like to hop and sing every day." She gets dressed and eats breakfast. After breakfast she hops and sings and watches TV. At 11:45 she goes back to sleep.

Ant walks home at lunch. She sees Grasshopper and says, "Hello!"

Grasshopper opens one eye and asks, "What time is it?"

Ant says, "It's 12:45."

Grasshopper sits up and smiles. "Is it time for lunch?" she asks.

"Yes," says Ant, "but you don't have any food."

The Two Brothers

Based on a
Middle Eastern Folktale
Retold by Judy Veramendi

In a town in the mountains there is a little family. The father is a doctor. The mother is a doctor. The two brothers in the family say, "We don't want to be doctors."

"What do you want to be?" asks the father.

The brothers say, "We always go for walks in the mountains. How about shepherds?"

1

When they get home their mother asks, "Do you like being shepherds?"

Big Brother says, "No! We can fight fires, fix teeth, help sick people, and teach sports."

"But we never want to be shepherds," says Little Brother.

4

The next day the two brothers go up the mountain. They find a shepherd with his sheep and he teaches them. "We can be shepherds!" they say.

After they eat lunch, they go to sleep under a tree.

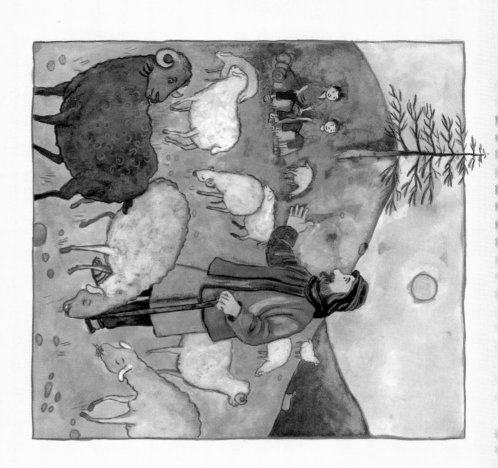

A horn pokes Big Brother in the arm. He jumps up and says to Little Brother, "Get up! Let's get out of here!" They do not look behind and see the sheep with horns.

They start to run down the mountain. Horns poke into them from behind. They cry, "Help!" They get to a river and swim.

"Help!"

City Mouse and Country Mouse

Based on a Greek Fable
Retold by Judy Veramendi

One day City Mouse takes a bus to the country to see his cousin, Country Mouse. He sees cows and horses in the fields. He sees ponds and fences and birds. The bus stops at a farm.

Country Mouse is waiting. "Hello, Cousin! I'm happy to see you," says Country Mouse.

But before they can eat, a big cat comes in. The cat wants to eat them! They have to hide behind the refrigerator.

Country Mouse says, "Now I'm hungry, and a cat wants to eat me! I'm going back to the country!"

But soon City Mouse is not happy. "I'm hungry. There is no food! And it's cold here in the barn," he says. "Let's go to the city. You can live in my apartment. There's food and it's warm."

Country Mouse touches his cold nose.

"Yes, let's go!" he says.

Oh, milk and cheese!

The two cousins take the bus to the city. They see a restaurant, a skating rink, and a museum. City Mouse says, "Here's our stop!" They get off the bus and go into the apartment. There are milk and cheese on a big table. City Mouse and Country Mouse are happy.

Why the Owl Says, "Who"

Based on a Southwestern U.S. Folktale
Retold by Judy Veramendi

There are many birds in the forest. Birds with red and green feathers sing in the trees. Birds with yellow and purple feathers come from the plains.

But there is one bird in the forest who has no feathers. She sits in a tree and cries, "I have no feathers!"

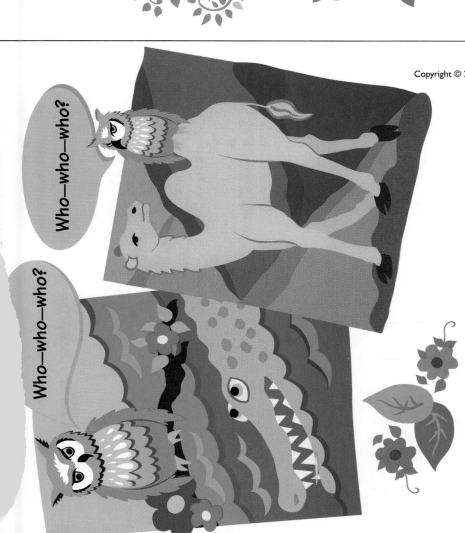

Who—who—who?

Who—who—who?

He asks the crocodile, who crawls in the river, "Who—who—who has my feather?" The crocodile doesn't know. He asks the camel, who walks in the desert, "Who—who—who has my feather?" The camel doesn't know.

To this day the owl says, "Who—who—who." He is always looking for his feather.

The birds in the forest say, "Let's help the bird with no feathers." The parrot gives her a red feather. The owl gives her a brown feather. Soon the sad bird gets five feathers, ten feathers, twenty feathers!

She laughs, "I don't need you. Now I have many feathers." And she flies out of the forest.

Who—who—who?

Who—who—who?

The owl is mad. He wants to find that bird. He wants his feather. He flies out of the forest.

He asks the monkey, who jumps in the jungle, "Who—who—who has my feather?" The monkey doesn't know. He asks the whale, who swims in the ocean, "Who—who—who has my feather?" The whale doesn't know.

Can We Go to the Beach Today?

by Judy Veramendi

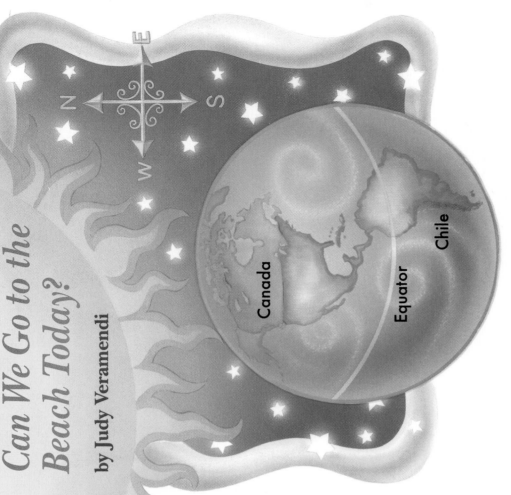

Chile is south of the equator. Canada is north of the equator. In Chile, it is summer in December. It is winter in June. But in Canada, it's the opposite. It's usually cold and snowy in December.

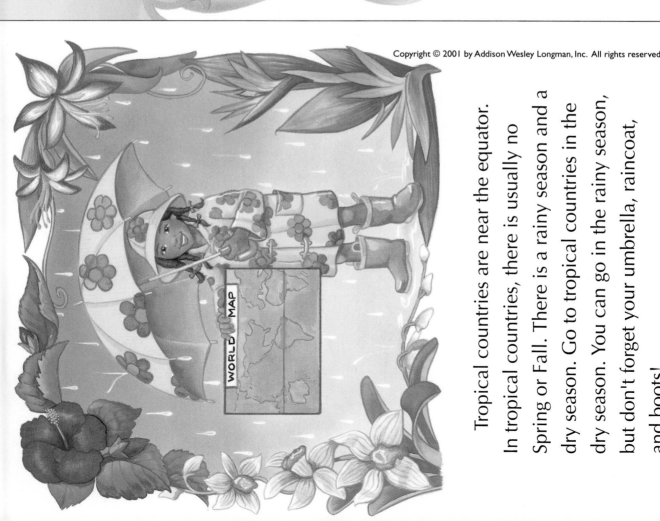

Tropical countries are near the equator. In tropical countries, there is usually no Spring or Fall. There is a rainy season and a dry season. Go to tropical countries in the dry season. You can go in the rainy season, but don't forget your umbrella, raincoat, and boots!

Do you like to go to the beach? You can go to the beach in July in Canada. And you can go to the beach in December in Chile.

Do you like to play in the snow? Go to Canada from December to March. Go to Chile from June to August. Bring your jacket, hat, gloves, and skis!

The Princess Can't Laugh

Based on an Irish Fairy Tale
Retold by Judy Veramendi

Yesterday Princess Eva was happy.
She went to a carnival. The weather
was sunny, and the food was delicious.
There were clowns and a band. But
there was a bad magician at the carnival.

Ha! Ha! Ha!

But then one day, a nice man came to
town. He had a band of animals. His dog,
his cat, and his horse sang for the princess.
They made loud noises. They sounded bad!
The princess started to laugh and laugh.
"Look! I can laugh! I can talk!" she cried.
It was a happy day.

Princess Eva saw the magician and she laughed. The magician didn't laugh. He touched her mouth with a wand. He said, "From now on, you can't talk. You can't laugh."

And Princess Eva couldn't make a sound.

Look at me!

Princess Eva could feel, and hear, and see, and smell, and taste. But she couldn't talk. She couldn't laugh. A doctor came and looked at her fingers, her ears, her eyes, her nose, and her tongue. She wasn't sick. But something was wrong. Even a clown couldn't make her laugh!

The Three Wishes

Based on an English Folktale
Retold by Judy Veramendi

One day a farmer goes to cut down a tree on his farm. The tree says, "Oh, farmer, please don't cut me down." The farmer stops.

The tree says, "Thank you! I am giving you and your family three wishes. You can have any three things you would like."

1

It smells like sausages!

Then the farmer and his father hear the mother at the door. "Use wish number three!" the father says.

"I'd like the sausages to disappear," the farmer says. Poof! The sausages disappear, along with the three wishes.

The mother comes in. "Good morning," she says. "It smells like sausages! Can I have some?"

4

The farmer runs into his house. His father is putting breakfast on the table. There are eggs, slices of tomato, toast and butter, and orange juice. The farmer says, "We have three wishes from a tree!" His father doesn't listen. "Sit down and enjoy your breakfast," says his father.

2

The farmer sits down and says, "Oh, I'd like sausages with my breakfast." Poof! And there is a bunch of sausages on his dish.

The father gets mad. "You wish for sausages?" he asks. "I'd like to see those sausages on your nose!" Poof! And the sausages are on the farmer's nose.

3

A Healthy Girl

by Judy Veramendi

Mai-Lan is from Vietnam. She lives in Chicago. Every day she eats fish and chicken. She likes rice and vegetables. And she loves salads. Her favorite fruits are apples and oranges. And she likes ice cream—chocolate ice cream!

Mai-Lan doesn't stay up late all the time. She did one time in the past year. Yesterday was the New Year celebration. Mai-Lan wanted to celebrate the New Year. She wanted to shout "Happy New Year!" with her family at midnight. And she did.

Mai-Lan likes to ride her bike. She loves to swim and go to the beach in the summer. On the playground, she jumps rope and plays games. Mai-Lan gets a lot of exercise. She's a healthy girl.

Usually Mai-Lan eats healthy foods, but yesterday she didn't. She ate a lot of candy. Usually she drinks milk and juice, but yesterday she didn't. She drank pop. Usually her bedtime is 9:00 P.M., but yesterday she didn't go to bed at 9:00. She stayed up past midnight!

Hello! My name is David. I live in Miami. My parents moved here when I was little. They're from Guatemala, and they speak Spanish. A lot of families in Miami speak Spanish. So there are a lot of Spanish TV shows.

Then I watched a cartoon show. Why? Because cartoons are my favorite shows! I awarded the cartoon show three stars.

There was a scary movie at 9:00. The TV reviewer awarded it four stars. But I didn't get to watch it. I did my homework. Then it was time for bed. In a few more years, I can watch late TV shows!

Last night I reviewed some TV shows for my school newspaper. I watched four kinds of shows. On the schedule at 7:00 was a comedy. The story was boring, but one character was funny. I awarded the comedy show one star.

Then there was a game show in Spanish. It was exciting and funny. I awarded it three stars. I'm happy I can speak Spanish and English. I can review a lot of shows! After the game show was a nature show. It was interesting enough. I awarded it two stars.

You may wish to use the HomeLink Readers for a family literacy program. Family members will enjoy learning to read the books along with children.

You may want to send this book home with the student as a homework activity book.

Teaching Instruction

Worksheets

HomeLink Readers 3 Worksheet Illustrations Mina Dolobowsky p. 45; Caroline Merola p. 41; Debbie Tilley p. 48.

Story Summary

A hardworking ant teaches a fun-loving grasshopper why it is important to work first and then play.

Word Bank

grasshopper, ant, breakfast, lunch

BEFORE READING

WARM UP

Model acting out activities the students do every day when they play. Invite them to join the actions, and then ask, "What are we doing?" Encourage answers such as, "We are playing soccer." Then repeat, using actions for work such as, "We are putting away library books."

PUT TOGETHER THE READER

Fold the pages in half to make the HomeLink Reader, *The Ant and the Grasshopper.*

PREVIEW THE READER

1. After the students have assembled the books, they can look at the pictures. Ask whether they think this story is real or make-believe.

2. Read the title aloud and lead a picture walk through the illustrations. Discuss what is happening on each page. Ask, "What is the ant doing? What is the grasshopper doing?" Encourage the students to identify objects and actions such as *soccer ball, watch, hopping, singing, sleeping,* and *food.* Ask the students to predict what they think the two characters are saying to each other.

SHARE WORDS

Write the Word Bank words on the board. Say each word and have the students say them after you. Ask the students to find these words in the HomeLink Reader. Then read the sentence in which the word appears.

DURING READING

READING

The students can listen as you read *The Ant and the Grasshopper* aloud. They can look at the illustrations as the story is read. Encourage questions and discussion of the story after it is read aloud.

GUIDED READING

Reread the story as the students follow along.

TEACHER/PARENT TIPS

Read a Grasshopper quote in a deep, smooth voice. Contrast with a high, nervous voice for Ant. Invite the students to imitate.

REREADING

Ask the students to recall their predictions about what the two characters were saying to each other. Compare their predictions with the actual events. Quickly summarize what the characters said to each other in the story. You may assess the students' comprehension with questions such as these:

Page 1 *What does Ant do before school?*
Page 2 *What does Grasshopper do after breakfast?*
Page 3 *At what time does Ant see Grasshopper?*
Page 4 *How does Ant help Grasshopper?*

Reread sections of dialogue to help the students answer the comprehension questions.

AFTER READING

Activities for Developing Language

SUMMARIZING

Reread each page of the story and have the students tell what happens page-by-page. Record the summaries. Then have the students complete this sentence to summarize the whole story: *An ant who works and works _____ a grasshopper to _____.*

ACT IT OUT!

Invite pairs to work together to act out the story. Provide props such as chairs, wristwatch, and soccer ball. You may wish to play the audio and have the students act out the actions as the story is read aloud.

ACTION CHARADES

Write these actions on slips of paper and put them in a container: *play soccer, watch TV, sing, hop, eat breakfast, go to sleep, work,* and *sit up.* Have partners choose a slip of paper and demonstrate the action dramatically. Ask the rest of the class to guess the action.

HOW DO WE GET FOOD?

Remind the students that ants gather the food they eat. Then turn the discussion to the ways people get the food they eat. The students may choose one food they like, such as pasta, and talk about how it gets to their plate—growing the wheat, making the pasta, putting it in a box, trucking it to the store, and selling it to the people who will eat it.

WRITE ABOUT IT!

Reread the last sentence of the story. Then ask the students to write what Grasshopper and Ant do after lunch. Invite them to draw a picture for each new word for their own Picture Dictionary.

GRAMMAR CONNECTION: POSSESSIVES

Write on the board the sentence *Grasshopper looks at Ant's food.* Ask who the food belongs to. Then point out how an apostrophe *s* (*'s*) tells us who something belongs to. Ask the students how they would say, "The soccer ball that belongs to Ant."

WORKSHEET

Students may complete the HomeLink Reader Comprehension sheet on page 40.

BULLETIN BOARD IDEAS

Put the title *How We Work and Play* on white chart paper. Invite the students to draw and display a mural of how they work and play each day.

FAMILY LITERACY

Invite the students to take the HomeLink Reader home and retell the story to their friends and family members. Suggest that the students ask them if they know this story.

Story Summary

Two brothers think they want to be shepherds until they go to the mountain, fall asleep and are chased by sheep, which they think are monsters.

Word Bank

mountains, shepherd, horns, father, mother, doctor

BEFORE READING

WARM UP

Invite the students to act out for the class what doctors, firefighters, dentists, and sports players do. Then ask the students to guess which occupation is being acted out.

PUT TOGETHER THE READER

Fold the pages in half to make the HomeLink Reader, *The Two Brothers.*

PREVIEW THE READER

1. After the students have assembled their books, have them look at the pictures. Ask them who the main characters are in the story.

2. Read the title aloud and have the students identify the two brothers. Then preview the pictures. Be sure the students realize that on page 3 the brothers are only imagining the monsters. Encourage the students to discuss what is happening on each page. Ask, "What does the father do for a living? Can you find the shepherd in the picture? How can you tell what the brothers are thinking?" Encourage the students to identify *shepherds, sheep, horns,* and *mountains.* Ask the students to predict why they think the two brothers are thinking about shepherds and sheep.

SHARE WORDS

Write the Word Bank words on the board. Ask the students to point to the words they know. Say each word. Then ask the students to say it after you and find a picture of it in their books.

DURING READING

READING

Invite the students to listen as you read the story aloud, looking at the illustrations as they listen. Tell them they will have a chance to ask questions and discuss the story after they hear it read aloud.

GUIDED READING

Reread the story as the students follow along. As you point to the words, encourage the students to point to the print.

TEACHER/PARENT TIPS

Invite the students to play the roles of the parents and the brothers on the first page and read aloud the dialogue. Encourage different tones of voice.

REREADING

Remind the students of their predictions. Quickly summarize the story events and compare them to the predictions. Check the students' comprehension with questions such as these:

Page 1 *What do the brothers want to be?*
Page 2 *How does the shepherd help the brothers?*
Page 3 *What are the two brothers scared of? What are really running after the brothers?*
Page 4 *What do the brothers think at the end of the story?*

Reread what the characters say on each page or point to the illustrations to help the students answer the comprehension questions.

AFTER READING

Activities for Developing Language

RETELL THE STORY

Reread the dialogue for the characters. Invite the students to take turns retelling what the characters say in their own words.

DRAWING CONCLUSIONS

Help the students draw conclusions by asking questions such as, "Why do you think the brothers want to be shepherds in the beginning of the story? Why do they think the sheep are monsters? Why don't they want to become shepherds at the end of the story?"

CONTEXT CLUES

Cover *pokes* and *poke* on page 3 and reread the page aloud, leaving out the words. Guide the students to understand they can figure out the missing words from picture clues and the words and sentences around the words. Uncover the *p* and tell the students they can also use the beginning letter sound to help them.

WHAT WE WANT TO BE

Invite the students to choose one job they would like to have when they grow up. They can work in small groups to draw a poster entitled *What We Want to Be*, illustrate it, and write captions.

ACT IT OUT!

Invite the students to act out the story. They can work in groups of seven, with two students playing the roles of the parents, two as the brothers, one as the shepherd, and two as the sheep. They can read the dialogue from the book or make up their own.

WRITE ABOUT IT!

Remind the students that the two brothers thought the sheep were monsters. Then ask them to recall a time when they thought they saw something, but it was really something else. Encourage the students to write about what they imagined and what was actually there. Then invite them to draw a picture for each new word for their own Picture Dictionary.

GRAMMAR CONNECTION: END PUNCTUATION

Remind the students that statements end in periods, questions end in question marks, and sentences that show strong expression end in exclamation marks. Help the students find examples of each in the story. Then ask them to read the sentences aloud with the correct tone of voice.

WORKSHEET

Students may complete the HomeLink Reader Comprehension sheet on page 41.

BULLETIN BOARD IDEAS

Using white chart paper, invite the students to display the pictures of what they want to be when they grow up. Title the bulletin board *What We Want to Be*.

FAMILY LITERACY

Encourage the students to share the HomeLink Reader at home with their friends and family members. Suggest that the students ask family members what they wanted to be when they were younger.

Story Summary

A city mouse and a country mouse visit each other, but neither mouse likes where the other mouse lives.

Word Bank

mouse, apartment, city, skating rink, restaurant, museum, barn, country, farm, field, cat, cow, horse, bird, pond, fence

BEFORE READING

WARM UP

Invite the students to pretend they are tiny mice and to act out situations such as these: *A mouse hides from the cat; The mouse is hungry; The mouse takes the bus.* After each action, ask, "What are you doing?" Guide the students to answer with complete sentences such as, "I am hiding from the cat."

PUT TOGETHER THE READER

Fold the pages in half to make the HomeLink Reader, *City Mouse and Country Mouse.*

PREVIEW THE READER

1. Ask the students to find the pictures of events that happen in the country. Then have them point to the ones that happen in the city.

2. Read the title aloud. Have the students first point to the mouse who lives in the city and then the one who lives in the country. Have the students tell what they see on each page. Ask, "How does City Mouse get to the country? What do the mice see in the country? What do the mice see that they like in the city? Why are the mice hiding?" Encourage the students to identify *cheese, bus, milk, country, mouse, cat,* and *refrigerator.* Ask the students to predict which place the mice like better, the city or country.

SHARE WORDS

Write the Word Bank words on the board. Ask volunteers to read any words they recognize. Then say each word and have the students say it after you. Then use each word in a sentence.

DURING READING

READING

Have students listen and follow the illustrations as you read the story aloud. Invite questions, and discuss the story after the students have heard it read aloud.

GUIDED READING

Reread the story as the students follow along. Point to the text as you read.

TEACHER/PARENT TIPS

Before the students read, ask if they have ever been to a place they didn't like. Then, as they read, have them decide if they like the city or country better.

REREADING

Review the story events as the students compare them with their predictions. Check the students' comprehension with questions such as these:

Page 1 *What does City Mouse see on the bus ride to visit his cousin?*
Page 2 *Why does City Mouse suggest they go to the city?*
Page 3 *What do the cousins see in the city?*
Page 4 *Why does Country Mouse want to go back to the country?*

As necessary, reread passages to help the students answer each comprehension question.

AFTER READING

Activities for Developing Language

COMPARE AND CONTRAST

Use a Venn diagram to contrast the two settings as shown in the story—the city and country. Then have the students use the diagram to tell how the country and city are alike and different.

DRAW CONCLUSIONS

Help the students draw conclusions about the characters by asking questions such as, "What do you think City Mouse thinks is more important—being warm or being safe? What do you think Country Mouse thinks is more important—having enough food or being safe?"

WORKING IN THE CITY AND COUNTRY

Display pictures of the city and the country and talk about what people do in both places. Have groups choose places to illustrate on a mural. The students should draw what people do in each place for work and play. After they draw their murals, invite them to tell the other group what they included in their drawings.

ACT IT OUT!

Partners may work together to act out the story. One student can pretend to be Country Mouse and the other can be City Mouse. Provide simple props such as two chairs for the bus.

WRITE ABOUT IT!

Remind the students of what both mice liked about the city and the country. Then have them brainstorm ideas about a vacation at a mouse hotel, complete with cheese, cats in cages, milk, bread, and a sunny warm beach. Suggest that the students draw a picture of the vacation place before they write a sentence about it. Invite them to draw a picture for each new word for their own Picture Dictionary.

GRAMMAR CONNECTION: CONTRACTIONS

Write the words *Here is* on the board and read the sentence on page 3, *Here's our stop!* Frame *Here's* and tell the students *Here's* is another way to say *Here is*. Show how the *i* is taken out and an apostrophe is added. Encourage the students to make up sentences with *Here is* and *Here's*.

WORKSHEET

Students may complete the HomeLink Reader Comprehension sheet on page 42.

BULLETIN BOARD IDEAS

You may wish to display a bulletin board of pictures of places the students know about and divide them into two sections under the titles, *City Places* and *Country Places*.

FAMILY LITERACY

Encourage the students to take the HomeLink Reader home to share with their friends and family members.

Story Summary

A featherless bird in the forest shows little thanks for the feathers the other birds give her. Owl goes in search of the thankless bird. Today he still says, "Who."

Word Bank

owl, feathers, cries, bird, camel, crocodile, whale, monkey, parrot, forest, jungle, ocean, plain, river, desert, crawl, walk, fly, jump, swim

BEFORE READING

WARM UP

Give one student a feather, or a drawing of a feather to pass along to another, who passes it on until you say, "Stop!" Explain that the student who has the feather should hide it behind his or her back. Ask the students one by one, "Who has the feather? Do you have the feather?" Have the students answer in complete sentences with "Yes" or "No" until you find the one with the feather.

PUT TOGETHER THE READER

Fold the pages in half to make the HomeLink Reader, *Why the Owl Says, "Who."*

PREVIEW THE READER

1. Tell the students to preview the pictures in their books. Encourage them to name the animals they recognize.

2. Read the title aloud. Then lead a picture walk through the illustrations, encouraging the students to tell what they see in each picture. Explain that this story will give the answer to the title. Ask, "What is the bird without feathers doing? What are the other birds doing to cheer up the bird without feathers?" Encourage the students to identify birds, feathers, and the colors they see. Ask the students to predict why they think the owl says, "Who."

SHARE WORDS

Write the Word Bank words on the board and say them aloud. Focus on each word and ask questions such as, "What word starts with *C* and is something you do when you are unhappy?"

DURING READING

READING

Invite the students to listen as you read the story aloud. Encourage them to look at the illustrations as they listen. Discuss the story after the students hear it read aloud.

GUIDED READING

As you reread the story, have the students follow along. Discuss how the illustrations can help them understand the text.

TEACHER/PARENT TIPS

During a rereading, have the students join in the refrain, *"Who-who-who has my feather?"*

REREADING

Remind the students of the predictions they made before they read the story. Quickly review the events in the story. Check the students' comprehension with questions such as these:

Page 1 *Why does one bird cry?*
Page 2 *What do the other birds do to help the bird without feathers?*
Page 3 *Why is the owl mad?*
Page 4 *Why does the owl still say, "Who" today?*

Reread dialogue and key passages as needed to help the students answer each comprehension question.

AFTER READING

Activities for Developing Language

CAUSE AND EFFECT

To help the students recognize cause-and-effect relationships, ask questions such as these: "Why does the bird cry? Why does the bird say, 'I don't need you' and fly away? Why does owl look for the bird?"

MAKING JUDGMENTS

Help the students make judgments about the characters, by asking questions such as these: "Do you think the birds were right to give the bird their feathers? Why or why not? Did the bird show her thanks when she got the feathers? Why do you think that? What could the bird have done to show her thanks?"

CLASSIFYING

Help the students classify the animals into categories, for example, animals that walk, fly, swim, and have feathers. Record the responses in a chart or list.

MAKE MASKS

List all the animals in the story on the board (*owl, monkey, whale, crocodile, camel, birds, bird without a feather*). Each student may choose an animal from the story and make a mask for that character. You may wish to hold an animal parade.

FIND OUT ABOUT OWLS

Invite interested students to find out more about owls. They can look at picture books about owls, watch a video, or read an encyclopedia entry. Each student may report to the class one interesting fact.

ACT IT OUT!

Invite groups to act out the story. They may wish to refer to the story, possibly using masks. The students may wish to refer to the story to remember dialogue or get ideas about what each character might say.

WRITE ABOUT IT!

Quickly review the ending of the story. Then ask the students to imagine that the owl found the bird who has his feather. Invite them to make up what the owl would say to the bird and how the bird would reply. Encourage the students to illustrate their writing and write the dialogue in speech balloons. Invite them to draw a picture for each new word for their own Picture Dictionary.

GRAMMAR CONNECTION: PRESENT TENSE

Remind the students that sentences that tell about what happens now are in the present tense. Write sentences such as the ones below on the board and have students point to the verbs that are in the present tense—happening now: *The owl flies out of the forest. The monkey jumps in the jungle. The bird sits in the tree and cries.*

WORKSHEET

Students may complete the HomeLink Reader Comprehension sheet on page 43.

BULLETIN BOARD IDEAS

You may wish to have each student choose a place where animals live, such as a forest, jungle, or pond, and draw a picture of the animals that live there. Arrange the drawings in a display titled *Animals and Where They Live*.

FAMILY LITERACY

Encourage the students to read the HomeLink Reader aloud at home. Then invite them to share the reactions of those at home in class.

Story Summary

Learn about weather at the equator and north and south of it. In Chile, it is summer in December. But in Canada, it is the opposite.

Word Bank

skis, equator, Chile, Canada, opposite, south, cold, rainy, snowy, tropical, beach, fall, spring, summer, winter

BEFORE READING

WARM UP

Provide assortments of clothes that might be worn outside in different temperatures and weather. The students might act out dressing for different weather. Ask them to identify the items they would be wearing for these weather conditions.

PUT TOGETHER THE READER

Fold the pages in half to make the HomeLink Reader, *Can We Go to the Beach Today?*

PREVIEW THE READER

1. Ask the students to tell what kind of weather they see in each picture.

2. Read the title aloud. Then preview the pictures with the students, reading aloud the labels for each page. Ask the students to describe what they see on each page and identify the weather. Ask, "What kind of day is it? Where is this picture taken? What are the people doing?" Help the students identify *beach, raincoat, rain, umbrella,* and *snow.* Ask the students to tell what they think they will learn about weather in this article.

SHARE WORDS

Write the Word Bank words on the board. Say them aloud and have the students repeat them after you. Help the students identify opposites. Locate the equator, Chile, and Canada on a globe.

DURING READING

READING

Call attention to the illustrations in the book as the students listen to an oral reading. Explain that they will be able to ask questions and discuss the story after it is read aloud.

GUIDED READING

Reread the story while the students follow along. Track the text as you read and encourage the students to do the same.

TEACHER/PARENT TIPS

Organize a choral reading of the text to highlight the contrasts. For example, on page 1, have Group 1 read sentences 1, 3, and 4, and have Group 2 read sentences 2, 5, and 6.

REREADING

Ask the students to tell something new they learned. Briefly summarize each page. Check the students' comprehension with questions such as:

Page 1 *In Canada, what starts in December?*
Page 2 *Where would you go to the beach in July?*
Page 3 *Where could you play in the snow in August?*
Page 4 *What two seasons do tropical countries have?*

AFTER READING:

Activities for Developing Language

PARAPHRASING

Read each page of the HomeLink Reader aloud. The students may take turns retelling each page in their own words.

MAIN IDEA

Write the sentences on page 4 on sentence strips. Display the first sentence. *(Tropical countries are near the equator.)* Tell the students this sentence is the main idea and tells what the paragraph is about. Then ask the students to read the other sentences. Help them realize that these sentences give details about the main idea. You might make a branched diagram to show how the details support the main idea.

CONTEXT CLUES

Point to the word *opposite* in the fifth sentence on page 1. Ask the students what the word means. Reread the other sentences in the paragraph and guide the students in using these sentences to help them figure out the meaning of the word. Discuss the contrasts between weather in Chile and Canada.

GIVE A WEATHER REPORT

Invite the students to choose a country and season and give a weather report for that day as a TV weatherperson might do. Encourage them to use a map of the country they choose.

WHERE CAN WE SKI?

Show a relief map of the world and help the students find mountainous areas where they would be able to ski. Begin the activity by pointing to a place in Canada, Colorado, or Chile.

WRITE ABOUT IT!

Show a weather report from yesterday's newspaper. Point out the high and low temperatures and other information given. Then invite the students to write a weather report for today. They can estimate the high and low temperatures and include other details such as rain, sun, or snow. The students may compare their weather reports with the newspaper the following day. Invite them to draw a picture for each new word for their own Picture Dictionary.

GRAMMAR CONNECTION: IMPERATIVE SENTENCES

Write these sentences on the board: *Go to Canada in December. Go to Chile in June. Bring your gloves. Play in the snow.* Then erase the verbs and write *Bring, Go, Play* on the board and ask the students to supply one of those words for each sentence. Add other sentences for the students to supply *Bring, Go,* or *Play.*

WORKSHEET

Students may complete the HomeLink Reader Comprehension sheet on page 44.

BULLETIN BOARD IDEAS

You may wish to have the students create a bulletin board entitled *Weather Around the World.* Encourage them to draw pictures with captions describing the weather.

FAMILY LITERACY

After the students have taken the HomeLink Reader home to read aloud, invite them to report on the reactions of their friends and family members.

Story Summary

A magician puts a spell on a princess so that she can't talk. But when a nice man comes to town and sings badly with his band of animals, she can laugh and speak again.

Word Bank

princess, magician, wand, weather, wrong, bad, carnival, clown, noise, happy

BEFORE READING

WARM UP

Write these words on slips of paper: *laugh, talk, sing, touch, hear, smell, feel, taste.* Have the students take turns choosing a slip of paper and acting out the words. Classmates can guess the action and the word for it. Encourage them to use complete sentences with the words they guess such as, "Ana is laughing."

PUT TOGETHER THE READER

Fold the pages in half to make the HomeLink Reader, *The Princess Can't Laugh.*

PREVIEW THE READER

1. Tell the students to look at the illustrations in the book. Ask them to point to the main character in the story.

2. Read the title aloud and walk through the illustrations with the students. Encourage them to tell what they see happening on each page. Ask, "Where is Princess Eva? How is she feeling on this page?" Encourage the students to identify *magician, princess, clowns,* and *animals.* Ask the students to predict what happens to Princess Eva.

SHARE WORDS

Write the Word Bank words on the board. Have the students point to any words they recognize. Say each word and have them say it after you. Use each word in a sentence.

DURING READING

READING

Ask the students to follow along in their books by looking at the illustrations as you read the story aloud. Discuss the story after it has been read.

GUIDED READING

Track the text as you reread the story and encourage the students to track with you as they follow along.

TEACHER/PARENT TIPS

On a rereading of the story, encourage the students to role-play the different characters as you read.

REREADING

Remind the students of their predictions and compare them to what actually happens in the story. Review what happens in the story. Check the students' comprehension with questions such as these:

Page 1 *Why do you think Princess Eva was happy?*
Page 2 *Why couldn't Princess Eva talk?*
Page 3 *What could Princess Eva do?*
Page 4 *What made Princess Eva laugh?*

As needed, reread key passages to help the students answer the comprehension questions.

AFTER READING

Activities for Developing Language

VISUALIZING

Reread page 1 as the students close their eyes. To help them imagine what is happening at the carnival, ask questions such as these: "What do you hear? How does the sun feel on your skin? What can you smell?"

PLOT

Draw three circles on the board and label them *Beginning, Middle,* and *End.* Ask the students to tell what happens in each part of the story. Then show how to use the chart to retell the story to a partner.

THE FIVE SENSES

Discuss the five senses and how Princess Eva experiences each in the story. Then help the students brainstorm other ways we experience each sense.

ACT IT OUT!

Invite the students to take the parts of Princess Eva, the magician, the clown, the nice man, the dog, the cat, and the horse. Encourage them to act out the story as you read it aloud and to improvise dialogue.

CARNIVAL TIME

Suggest that the students draw a picture of a carnival they have attended or heard about. Encourage them to display pictures and describe them to their classmates. Ask that they tell what might go on at a carnival, what kinds of food there might be, and why a carnival might be held.

WRITE ABOUT IT!

Reread the last page of the story. Then invite the students to imagine what Princess Eva said to the nice man and his animals after she found she could speak again and how the nice man replied. They might use play format or quotation marks. Invite them to draw a picture for each new word for their own Picture Dictionary.

GRAMMAR CONNECTION: SIMPLE PAST OF *GO (WENT)*

Write sentences on the board such as these: *Today the Princess and a bad magician go to the carnival.* Have the students change *today* to *yesterday* and change the verb tense from present to the past.

WORKSHEET

Students may complete the HomeLink Reader Comprehension sheet on page 45.

BULLETIN BOARD IDEAS

Help the students create a bulletin board entitled *The Five Senses* that will have their drawings of how they experience the world through touch, smell, taste, sound, and sight.

FAMILY LITERACY

Encourage the students to take the HomeLink Reader home and share it with their friends and family members.

Story Summary

A farmer and his father foolishly waste three wishes at breakfast. And the mother thinks she smells sausages!

Word Bank

disappear, sausages, wish, number, farmer, butter, egg, orange juice, toast, tomato, slice, breakfast

BEFORE READING

WARM UP

Invite the students to role-play ordering breakfast at a restaurant with you as waiter. Write the orders on sheets of paper. Then have the students read the orders back to other students and ask them if the orders are correct.

PUT TOGETHER THE READER

Fold the pages in half to make the HomeLink Reader, *The Three Wishes*.

PREVIEW THE READER

1. Invite the students to look at the illustrations in the book. Ask them to identify the food items on each page.

2. Read the title aloud and preview the illustrations with the students. Discuss what they see happening on each page. Ask, "What is the farmer doing? What is the farmer having for breakfast? Why do you think the sausage is on the farmer's nose?" Encourage the students to identify *sausage, farmer,* and *tree*. Ask them to predict what the three wishes will be.

SHARE WORDS

Write the Word Bank words on the board. Have the students point to any words they recognize. Say each word and have the students say it after you. Then say the meaning of each word and have the students point to the corresponding word.

DURING READING

READING

As the students look at the illustrations in their books, read the story aloud. Remind the students they will be able to ask questions and discuss the story after they hear it read aloud.

GUIDED READING

Reread the story as the students follow along. Show how to follow the words you are reading by tracking as you read.

TEACHER/PARENT TIPS

Reread the story aloud and have groups of students fill in by reading the direct words of the father and the farmer.

REREADING

Review the students' predictions and compare them to what actually happens in the story. Provide a quick review. Check the students' comprehension with questions such as these:

Page 1 *Why does the tree give the farmer three wishes?*
Page 2 *What is the farmer's father doing?*
Page 3 *How do the farmer and his father use the first two wishes?*
Page 4 *How does the farmer use the last wish?*

Reread dialogue that might help the students answer each comprehension question.

AFTER READING

Activities for Developing Language

CHARACTER

Discuss with the students the character of the farmer and his father. Use a character web to record their responses. Prompt them with questions such as, "Is the farmer kind to the tree? Does the father listen? Is the father patient? Does the father lose his temper with the farmer? Who is foolish in this story?"

MAKING JUDGMENTS

To help the students make judgments about what the characters do and say in the story, ask, "Do you think the farmer was wise not to cut down the tree? How could the farmer have used his first wish more wisely? Was the farmer's father wise to wish the sausages were on the farmer's nose? Do you think the farmer's last wish was wise?"

PLOT

Create a story map by dividing chart paper into five boxes with the headings *Character, Setting, Problem, Events,* and *Solution.* Then have the students work with you to fill in the different boxes. They can use the story map to retell the story.

A HEALTHY BREAKFAST

Display a food pyramid and discuss the foods we need to eat each day in order to be healthy. Then have the students make a list of foods that would make a healthy breakfast.

A FARMER'S JOB

Discuss what a farmer does for a living. Display pictures of farmers at work to stimulate discussion or invite a guest speaker to the classroom to speak and answer questions.

WRITE ABOUT IT!

Invite the students to write three wishes of their own. Suggest that they illustrate the wishes by showing what could happen once the wishes were granted.

GRAMMAR CONNECTION: DIALOGUE

Explain that quotation marks in a story mean a person is speaking those words. Compare quotation marks to speech balloons. Have the students find the dialogue in the story and read it aloud. Point out the tags, such as *he says.* Then have the students write something the farmer might say to his mother when she asks for sausages and include quotation marks in the dialogue.

WORKSHEET

Students may complete the HomeLink Reader Comprehension sheet on page 46.

BULLETIN BOARD IDEAS

Invite the students to display drawings and text on a bulletin board entitled *My Three Wishes.*

FAMILY LITERACY

Encourage the students to take the HomeLink Reader home to share with their friends and family members.

Story Summary

Mai-Lan is a healthy girl most of the time. She eats good food, gets plenty of rest, and exercises—except when she celebrates the New Year.

Word Bank

Vietnam, Chicago, bedtime, exercise, fruit, healthy, vegetable

BEFORE READING

WARM UP

Invite the students to brainstorm things they do every day to keep healthy. List their ideas on the board. Then have them choose one thing and act it out with a partner. Ask, "What are you doing?" The students then might answer, "We are jumping rope."

PUT TOGETHER THE READER

Fold the pages in half to make the HomeLink Reader, *A Healthy Girl.*

PREVIEW THE READER

1. Call attention to the illustrations in the book. Ask students who they think the main character is. Ask them to point to illustrations showing how the girl keeps healthy.

2. Read the title aloud and have the students preview the illustrations. Talk about what they see on each page. Ask, "What is the girl doing? What kind of exercise is the girl doing?" Encourage the students to name *bike, beach bag, apples,* and *pop* as you point to the words. Ask the students to predict what they think the girl in the story will do.

SHARE WORDS

Write the Word Bank words on the board and say them aloud. Use each word in a sentence. On a world map, point out where Chicago and Vietnam are.

DURING READING

READING

Ask the students to look at the illustrations in their books as you read the story aloud. Explain that they will be able to ask questions and discuss the story after they hear it read aloud.

GUIDED READING

As the students follow along, reread the story, pointing to the print as you read.

TEACHER/PARENT TIPS

Reread the story aloud, pausing before key words so the students can say them. For example, ask the students to supply *fruits, ice cream, healthy,* and *yesterday.*

REREADING

Help the students recall their predictions and compare them to what actually happened in the story. Quickly recap what the story is about. Check the students' comprehension with questions such as these:

Page 1 *What foods does Mai-Lan like?*
Page 2 *What does Mai-Lan do to get exercise?*
Page 3 *What did Mai-Lan do that is not healthy?*
Page 4 *Why did Mai-Lan change her health habits on this one day?*

As necessary, reread key passages or whole pages to help the students answer comprehension questions.

AFTER READING

Activities for Developing Language

COMPARE AND CONTRAST

Invite the students to make a list of foods they like to eat. List them on the board. Then draw a Venn diagram. Use the diagram to compare and contrast the foods they like with the ones Mai-Lan likes.

MAKING JUDGMENTS

To help the students make judgments about what Mai-Lan does, ask, "Why do you think Mai-Lan eats healthy foods? Do you think it is all right for Mai-Lan to stay up late and eat candy one night a year? What do you think would happen if Mai-Lan made a habit of staying up late and eating a lot of candy?"

CAUSE AND EFFECT

To help the students recognize cause-and-effect relationships, ask, "Why does Mai-Lan eat fruits and vegetables? Why does Mai-Lan go to bed at nine o'clock? Why did Mai-Lan stay up yesterday? Why did Mai-Lan eat candy yesterday?"

MAKE A FOOD PYRAMID

Invite the students to use old magazines and cut out pictures of foods in the different food groups. Draw a large food pyramid on chart paper. The students may then fill in the pyramid with the foods they cut out and then label each picture.

WAYS TO CELEBRATE

Invite the students to draw a picture that shows how they celebrate each New Year's Day with their families and friends. Then have them share their pictures with their classmates.

WRITE ABOUT IT!

Ask the students to make a list of their five favorite foods and write a sentence about one of the foods. Encourage students to share their lists with their classmates. Invite them to draw a picture for each new word for their own Picture Dictionary.

GRAMMAR CONNECTION: CONTRACTIONS

Write these sentences on the board:

> Mai-Lan did not go to school today.
> Mai-Lan didn't go to school today.

Point to *didn't* and explain that it is a contraction. Ask the students to find the two words in the first sentence that *didn't* stands for. Write *did not* on the board. Take out the *o* and replace it with an apostrophe. Then ask the students to say the new word. Repeat the procedure, using *do not* and *don't*.

WORKSHEET

Students may complete the HomeLink Reader Comprehension sheet on page 47.

BULLETIN BOARD IDEAS

Help the students create a bulletin board titled *Our Favorite Healthy Foods* for displaying their drawings and writings about the food they like.

FAMILY LITERACY

Invite the students to take the HomeLink Reader home. Encourage them to share the book with their friends and family members.

Story Summary

David reviews TV programs in Spanish and English for his school newspaper. He likes game shows and nature shows, but cartoon shows are his favorites.

Word Bank

awarded, newspaper, Guatemala, Miami, families, Spanish, character, review, movie, story

BEFORE READING

WARM UP

Invite each student to pretend to be a TV or movie character by acting out something that character is likely to do or say. Then have the class guess the character's identity.

PUT TOGETHER THE READER

Fold the pages to make the HomeLink Reader, *TV in Two Languages.*

PREVIEW THE READER

1. Help the students find Guatemala and Miami on the map illustration. Then ask them to point to the main character in the book.

2. Read the title aloud and have the students look at the illustrations and tell what they see the main character doing. Ask, "Why is the boy writing? How does the boy feel as he watches the shows?" Ask the students to predict why they think the boy is pointing to the globe.

SHARE WORDS

After writing the Word Bank words on the board, ask the students to point to any words they know. Say all the words aloud and have the students repeat them after you. Then use each word in a sentence.

DURING READING

READING

Explain that it will help the students understand the story to look at the illustrations as they listen to you read the story aloud. Invite questions and discussion.

GUIDED READING

As you reread the story, use your finger to track the print. Encourage the students to follow along, also tracking as they read.

TEACHER/PARENT TIPS

Have the students read each sentence in unison after you read, modeling the most effective intonation appropriate to the sentence.

REREADING

Review the students' predictions and compare them to the content of the story. Give a brief review of what happens in the story. Check the students' comprehension with questions such as:

Page 1 *Who is telling this story?*
Page 2 *What did David do for his school newspaper?*
Page 3 *What show did David like more, the nature show or game show?*
Page 4 *What can David do in a few years?*

As needed, reread or frame key passages to help the students answer each comprehension question.

AFTER READING

Activities for Developing Language

CLASSIFY

Write these categories on the board: *Comedy, Cartoon, Nature Show, Movie, Game Show.* Then invite the students to suggest TV shows or movies that fit each category.

MAIN IDEA AND DETAILS

Write the sentences from page 2 on sentence strips. Help the students identify one sentence that tells the main idea *(Last night I reviewed some TV shows for my school newspaper.)* and the other sentences that tell details about the main idea.

FACT AND OPINION

Tell the students that sentences that can be proved true or false are facts. Sentences that tell what someone thinks or feels are opinions. Ask the students to reread pages 2 and 3 and to find a sentence on each page that is an opinion and one that is a fact.

MATH CONNECTION

Suggest that students make a time line from 7:00 P.M. to 9:00 P.M. Then have them list the shows that David watched or could have watched from seven o'clock until he went to bed at nine o'clock.

SOCIAL STUDIES CONNECTION

Help the students locate where they live on a world map. Then have them find Miami. Ask the students to identify the state and country where they find Miami. Outline South America with a pointer and ask them to locate Guatemala and its capital.

WRITE ABOUT IT!

Ask the students to write a review of a TV show they have seen in the past week. Tell them to name the show, tell when it is on TV, who the main characters are, what the show was about, and why they liked it or disliked it.

GRAMMAR CONNECTION: ANSWER QUESTIONS IN THE PAST TENSE

Write these questions on the board and read them aloud: *Where did David's parents move when he was little? What did David do last night? What did David watch first?* After the students answer each question, write the response on the board and underline the past tense verb.

WORKSHEET

Students may complete the HomeLink Reader Comprehension sheet on page 48.

BULLETIN BOARD IDEAS

You may wish to have the students create a bulletin board titled *Our Favorite TV Shows* to display pictures of their TV shows, their written reviews, and TV show advertisements.

FAMILY LITERACY

Encourage the students to take the HomeLink Reader home and share it with their friends and family members.

The Ant and the Grasshopper

1. Circle. Draw.

Do you like Ant or Grasshopper? Draw the one you like.

Ant   **Grasshopper**

2. Write.

1. What does Ant do before she goes to school?

_____

_____

2. What does Grasshopper do after lunch?

_____

_____

Students draw the character they like from the story.
They answer questions about the characters.

The Two Brothers

1. **Draw.**

    What do you want to be?

2. **Look at the picture.**

    Write the sentence. Number the sentences.

     ____ _____

     ____ _____

     ____ _____

Students draw what they would like to be. They write sentences
that describe the pictures and number them in order.

City Mouse and Country Mouse

1. Circle. Draw.

Do you like the city or the country?

City   **Country**

[blank drawing box]

2. Write.

    1. Does City Mouse like the country? Why?

    _____

    _____

    2. Does Country Mouse like the city? Why?

    _____

    _____

Students draw the city or the country. They answer questions about the characters in the story.

Why the Owl Says, "Who"

1. **Draw the bird with no feathers.**   **Draw her after she gets 20 feathers.**

2. **Write.**

   1. Why is the owl mad?

   _____

   _____

   _____

   2. Where can the owl look for his feather?

   _____

   _____

   _____

Students draw two pictures. They draw the bird with
no feathers. They draw her after she gets 20 feathers.
They answer questions about the owl.

Can We Go to the Beach Today?

1. Circle. Draw.

Would you like to be in Chile in June or December?

June   **December**

2. Write.

1. When is a good time to go to the beach in Canada? Why?

_____

_____

_____

2. When is a good time to go to the beach in Chile? Why?

_____

_____

_____

Students circle and draw Chile in June or December.
They answer questions about when to go to the beach.

The Princess Can't Laugh

1. Draw Princess Eva. She can't laugh or talk.

Write. What is she thinking?

[empty box]

2. Write the sentences.

Number the sentences.

 _____.

 _____.

 _____.

Students draw Princess Eva when she can't talk or laugh
and write what she is thinking. They write sentences that
describe illustrations and number them.

The Three Wishes

1. **Draw a magic tree.**
   Write a wish.

2. **Circle. Write.**
   What wishes are in the story?

   I'd like bananas for breakfast.

   I'd like sausages with my eggs.

   I'd like to see those sausages on your nose.

   I'd like toast with fruit.

   I'd like the sausages on my nose to disappear.

   _____

   _____

   _____

Students draw a magic tree and write a wish.
They circle the wishes from the story and write them.

A Healthy Girl

1. Draw.

What makes Mai-Lin a healthy girl?

2. Tell about Mai-Lin.

1. What does Mai-Lin usually drink?

   _____

2. What time does Mai-Lin usually go to bed?

   _____

3. Tell about you.

1. What time do you usually go to bed?

   _____

2. What time do you go to bed on special nights?

   _____

Students draw Mai-Lin's healthy habits.
They answer questions about Mai-Lin
and about themselves.

TV in Two Languages

1. Draw a line.

How many stars does David give each show?

game show

nature show

comedy show

cartoon show

 ★   ★★   ★★★

2. Write.

1. What is your favorite kind of TV show? Why?

_____

_____

2. Write a review of a TV show.

_____

_____

Students match type of TV show to the stars David gave it. They tell what kind of TV show they like and review a TV show.